SPECTRUM FOCUS

MW01260149

Reading for Main Ideas and Details in Informational Text
Grade 4

Table of Contents

Free Video Tutorial

 Use this QR code to launch a short video that provides instruction for skills featured in this book. To access the video from your smartphone or tablet:

- Download a free QR code scanner from your device's app store.
- Launch the scanning app on your device.
- Scan the code to visit the web page for this book.
- Find the video under the Resources tab.

This *Spectrum Focus* video is also available at:
- http://www.carsondellosa.com/704907
- www.youtube.com/user/CarsonDellosaPub

Spectrum®
An imprint of Carson-Dellosa Publishing LLC
P.O. Box 35665
Greensboro, NC 27425

© 2016 Carson-Dellosa Publishing LLC. Except as permitted under the United States Copyright Act, no part of this publication may be reproduced, stored, or distributed in any form or by any means (mechanically, electronically, recording, etc.) without the prior written consent of Carson-Dellosa Publishing LLC. Spectrum® is an imprint of Carson-Dellosa Publishing LLC.

Printed in the USA • All rights reserved.

ISBN 978-1-4838-2423-9

02-226157784

Focus On Reading for Main Ideas and Details

The ability to understand informational texts is an essential skill. Our world is full of nonfiction texts, including articles, websites, manuals, directions, maps, charts, and many more. When reading nonfiction, readers must learn to locate important details, to deduce or *infer* information that is not directly stated, to determine the main idea, and to decide whether ideas are well-supported by key details. For each of these skills, *Reading for Main Ideas and Details in Informational Text* provides step-by-step teaching, explanations, and practice. Close reading of short nonfiction passages is followed by text-based comprehension questions that build critical-thinking skills.

Read this text closely. It will be used to illustrate the topics that follow.

Insect Senses

1   Did you know that insects see, feel, and taste, just as people do? They use their senses to collect information from the environment. This information goes to the brain or nervous system and helps insects decide how to behave. Insect bodies come in an amazing range of shapes, sizes, colors, and forms. Because insects have a wide variety of sense organs, they have amazing sensory abilities.

2   Many insects use compound eyes to see. These eyes are made up of separate sections called *ommatidia*. Each section points in one direction and contains a lens and light-sensitive cells. The eyes of some species have thousands of sections. Compound eyes create pictures that are mosaics of dots, with each dot coming from one section. Higher quality pictures are produced by compound eyes with more sections.

3   All insects have a pair of sensory organs called *antennae*. These segmented stalks are usually located on the head above or between the eyes. There are at least 15 different types of antennae. They are used to feel and to detect odors, wind speed, heat, and moisture. Antennae may also grasp prey.

4   Insects also have taste receptors. Most insects taste with their mouths. However, butterflies and flies have taste receptors on their feet! Honeybees have tasting organs on the tips of their antennae. These receptors trap chemicals in solid and liquid foods. Then, nearby nerve cells send signals to the animal's brain.

5   There are over one million species of insects, and each one has unique abilities. Insects have a variety of sense organs that allow them to see the world in strange and surprising ways. The next time you look at a flower, feel a blade of grass, or taste some sweet fruit, stop and think about how insects experience the world we share.

Using Details to Answer Questions

Readers are often asked to answer questions about a text to show their understanding. You may need to answer questions like these during a class discussion, for homework, or on a test.

When explaining what an informative text says, refer to details and examples. If you read an article about how to make maple syrup and miss details about what type of tree is needed (sugar maple trees) or during what time of year syrup is made (February and March), then you haven't understood the text well.

Most questions about informative texts can be answered by closely reading exactly what the text says. To answer some questions, readers will need to put details together from several different spots in the text. Other questions require readers to compare one part of the text to another part. Look at these examples.

2   Many insects use compound eyes to see. These eyes are made up of separate sections called *ommatidia*. Each section points in one direction and contains a lens and light-sensitive cells. The eyes of some species have thousands of sections. Compound eyes create pictures that are mosaics of dots, with each dot coming from one section. Higher quality pictures are produced by compound eyes with more sections.

What is an *ommatidia*? An ommatidia is one section of an insect's compound eye.

Give two examples of insect sense organs. Two insect sense organs are compound eyes and antennae.

3   All insects have a pair of sensory organs called *antennae*. These segmented stalks are usually located on the head above or between the eyes. There are at least 15 different types of antennae. They are used to feel and to detect odors, wind speed, heat, and moisture. Antennae may also grasp prey.

Antennae are sensitive to moisture. What are the cells in compound eyes sensitive to? They are sensitive to light.

Focus On Reading for Main Ideas and Details

Using Details to Draw Inferences

The answers to some questions cannot be found directly in the text. To arrive at an answer, readers must use what they have read in addition to what they already know to fill in missing information. Answering a question in this way is called *drawing an inference.*

An *inference* is a conclusion based on evidence. If the evidence is weak, the conclusion may be incorrect. When making an inference, first look at evidence from the text. Make sure you understand facts, details, and examples from the text before you decide what is missing. Then, think about other sources of information. Evidence can come from personal experience and general knowledge about the world, from other texts you have read, and from logical thinking. Putting all this evidence together will help you draw good inferences.

Imagine you are reading a website about how to play a card game. The question on your mind is: *Would my five-year-old brother like to play this game?* To decide, carefully read details about the game. Then, think about what your brother is able to do and what he enjoys. The evidence should help you make a good inference. Look at more examples of inferences related to "Insect Senses."

Question: Why is it helpful for butterflies to taste with their feet?

Evidence: The text says that butterflies have taste receptors on their feet. I have seen butterflies land on flowers with their feet. I remember reading that butterflies drink nectar from flowers.

Inference: It is helpful for butterflies to taste with their feet because they can find out if a flower's nectar will be good to drink as soon as they land on it.

Question: How could information from an insect's antennae help it decide how to behave?

Evidence: The text states that information from sense organs helps insects decide how to behave. It also says that antennae can detect (or provide information about) heat in the environment. I have seen insect behaviors such as walking and flying.

Inference: An insect's antennae might provide the information that there is something hot nearby. This would help the insect decide to walk or fly in the other direction.

Finding the Main Idea

The *main idea* is the most important idea that an author wants readers to understand. Finding the main idea is more than just explaining what a text is about. Instead, it is finding the "big idea" that you remember long after reading.

Main ideas can be about anything, but they often fall into these categories.

The main idea tells how to do something or describes a process.	Example: *It is easy to make a kite at home.*
The main idea explains what causes an event.	Example: *When pressure builds up in melted rock under Earth's surface, a volcano can erupt.*
The main idea gives a solution to a problem.	Example: *Westside School should spend more of its budget on new computers.*
The main idea compares ideas, events, or things.	Example: *Although they are both levels of the ocean, the sunlight zone and the twilight zone are like different worlds.*
The main idea tells how different ideas or examples are related.	Example: *Insects have a variety of sense organs that allow them to see the world in strange and surprising ways.*

Sometimes, a reader has to infer the main idea. However, in many informational texts, the author states the main idea clearly. Look at the final example in the chart above. Do you recognize it? It comes directly from the last paragraph of "Insect Senses." It clearly states the main idea of the entire text.

Finding Key Details that Support the Main Idea

All the facts, details, and examples in an informational text help to explain and support the main idea. *Key details* are the main details that give reasons and examples of why the main idea is true and important. Think of key details from the text as rungs on a ladder. The main idea is at the top of the ladder.

Key details in the text on page 2 support the main idea "Insects have a variety of sense organs that allow them to see the world in strange and surprising ways." This main idea is stated in the first paragraph and restated in the last paragraph. Each of the paragraphs in between, or *body paragraphs*, contains a key detail to support this main idea. The key detail is often the first sentence in a paragraph.

• In paragraph 2, the key detail is "Many insects use compound eyes to see." This is a main example of an insect sense organ that lets insects experience the world. The rest of the details in this paragraph explain how compound eyes work. These less important details are not key details.

- In paragraph 3, the key detail is "All insects have a pair of sensory organs called *antennae*." It gives another main example of an insect sensory organ.

- In paragraph 4, the key detail is "Insects also have taste receptors." This main detail supports the main idea by giving another example of a type of insect sensory organ. The rest of the details in this paragraph support this key detail by explaining different kinds of taste receptors and how they work.

Using Details to Explain Events and Ideas

Many nonfiction texts contain complex and detailed information. A news article might explain all the events that led up to the creation of a new country. A science book might describe stages in the life of a star. A website might give step-by-step instructions for installing an app.

After reading a text that includes many details, test yourself to see how well you understood it. See if you can describe an event, procedure, or idea from the text in your own words. Try to explain what happens and why it happens that way. To do this, readers need to have a complete understanding of the details in a text and how they fit together to support the main idea.

Look at the questions below. To answer them, a reader must have a solid understanding of the text on page 2. The sample answers are in a student's own words. They are based on details from the text.

Question: Explain how a fly might taste a rotting apple.

Answer: When the fly lands on the apple, chemicals from the apple will enter the taste receptors on the fly's feet. The fly's brain will get the message that the apple is good to eat. The fly will probably eat some of the apple.

Question: Explain how an ant might feel a rock in its path.

Answer: As the ant walks along, its antennae would feel and sense things near its head. The ant's antennae would feel the rock. They might also sense whether the rock was wet or dry, or hot or cold. When the ant's antennae feel the rock, the ant might decide to go around it or over it.

Summarizing a Text

Summarizing is a skill that most people use every day. When someone asks you how your day was, you usually don't list every little thing that happened. Instead, you give a summary of the day's most important or interesting events. You do the same thing when you give someone a recap or summary of a movie, book, or sporting event. A good summary gives the "gist" of the text. It includes the key ideas and main points. It leaves out less important details and information.

Readers are often asked to summarize what they read in informational texts. Good readers keep a running summary in their heads as they read, making a mental note when they read information that seems especially important or interesting. To write a summary, first use the five **W**s and **H** to ask questions about a text. Look at these example questions and answers about "Insect Senses."

Who or what is the text about?	It is about insects.
What information is most important?	Important information is given about how insects see, feel, and taste.
When does something important happen?	Insects use their senses when they need to decide how to behave.
Where does something important happen?	Insects use their senses to experience the world.
Why is this topic important?	This topic is important because insects' sense organs and sensory abilities are unusual and interesting.
How does something important happen?	Insects use compound eyes, antennae, and taste receptors to see, feel, and taste.

The answers to these questions provide important information to include in a summary. A summary of a short passage like the one on page 2 should be about one paragraph (or three to five sentences) long. Read the example summary below.

Insects have unusual sense organs that help them gather information about the environment in interesting ways. They use compound eyes to see, antennae to feel, and taste receptors to taste food. An insect's senses help it experience the world and make decisions about how to behave.

Informational Text Finding Details

Read the text. Use it to answer the questions on pages 9 and 10.

Bread: An International Food

1   Do you eat bread every day? If you are like many people, the answer is *yes*. Even if you don't eat sliced bread each day, you probably eat bread in other forms—as rolls, bagels, muffins, crackers, tortillas, or pizza crusts. In this way, you are like people around the world. In almost every culture and every country, people enjoy bread as a *staple* (essential part) of their diets.

2   To make bread, you need only flour and water. Flour is commonly made from grains of wheat, oats, rye, cornmeal, millet, quinoa, or rice. Many breads also contain yeast. Yeast are living microscopic fungi cells that change sugar into other chemicals. As the yeast does its work, the bread dough rises. Dough is shaped into loaves, squares, circles, or rings. It can be baked, grilled, boiled, or fried.

3   Every day in Asia, people eat bread. In India, people enjoy *chapati* cooked on a griddle called a *tawa* or crisp *naan* baked in an oven called a *tandoor*. In China, dough is often steamed to make soft, puffy rolls. In Singapore, people eat *roti jala*, a bread full of holes. Its name comes from the word for a fisherman's net.

4   Every day in Africa, people eat bread. Moroccans eat *pita bread* with delicious fillings stuffed inside. South Africans make *green mealie bread* from steamed corn. In Nigeria, *puff puff*, or balls of fried dough, is popular. Ethiopians enjoy *injera* cooked in flat rounds so large that they double as plates!

5   Every day in Europe, people eat bread. *Focaccia* is a savory Italian bread first made by ancient Romans. A loaf of *Irish soda bread*, called a *cake*, is made with salt, buttermilk, and baking soda. On Easter, Russians eat sweet *kulich* baked in tall cylindrical molds. In German kitchens, dark-colored *rye bread* is a favorite.

6   Every day in North America and South America, people eat bread. In Mexico, people celebrate *Día de los Muertos*, or the Day of the Dead, with licorice-flavored *pan de muerto*. Venezuelan *pan de jamón* is rolled around ham and raisins. Many Native Americans eat *fry bread* when they gather at festivals.

7   What type of bread is your favorite? The next time you eat a sandwich or munch on a quesadilla, think of people sitting down together for meals around the world. Chances are, they are eating bread, too!

Guided Practice Finding Details

I. What two ingredients are required for making bread?

> Understanding how an informational text is organized will help you quickly locate details that will help you answer a question like this one. Each paragraph in the text on page 8 explains something about bread. Can you find the paragraph that is about how bread is made? Paragraph 2 gives details about bread making. If you reread it, you will probably find a detail that answers the question. Before you write your answer, go back and reread the question. It asks for "two ingredients." Does the detail you found mention two ingredients? If it does, you are ready to answer. If not, keep searching.

Now, write your answer as a complete sentence.

_____

_____

2. What is one type of bread eaten in Italy?

> A time-consuming way to find a detail that answers this question would be to look back at each country mentioned in the text until you find Italy. A shorter way would be to use background knowledge (or a map) to remember that Italy is on the continent of Europe. Several paragraphs in the text focus on bread in different continents of the world. One paragraph (paragraph 5) is about Europe. Reread it for any details about Italy. Then, read the question again to make sure you can answer it correctly and completely. The question mentions "Italy," but the detail in the text says "Italian." Do this noun and adjective match? If they do, you are ready to answer the question. If not, keep searching.

Write your answer as a complete sentence.

_____

_____

_____

Independent Practice Finding Details

1. What are seven grains that can be used to make flour for bread?

   _____   _____

   _____   _____

   _____   _____

   _____

2. What are two types of bread eaten for holidays and special occasions? Describe the countries and special days associated with each one.

   _____

   _____

   _____

3. What bread gets its name from the word for a fisherman's net? Why?

   _____

   _____

   _____

4. Indian naan bread is baked in a
   A. fisherman's net.   **B.** tandoor.
   C. millet.   **D.** chapati.

5. Circle two words that do not name a type of bread.

   puff puff   injera   tortillas   yeast   tawa   kulich

6. Write the missing step for making yeast bread.
   - Microscopic fungi cells called *yeast* are added to bread dough ingredients.
   - _____
   - Bread dough rises.

Informational Text Drawing Inferences

Read the text. Use it to answer the questions on pages 12 and 13.

Life as a Mummy

1   Humans have always had many ideas about what happens after death. The ancient Egyptians believed that after a person died, he or she would journey to another world and live again. They believed that bodies needed to be preserved. That way, they could be used in the afterlife. Ancient Egyptian mummies are a useful source of information about life long ago. They help us learn what the Egyptians believed and what they valued.

2   Mummifying a body was not a quick or simple process. In fact, it took about 70 days from start to finish. The first step was to remove the organs. The only organ left behind was the heart. The Egyptians believed that this is where the soul was found. They thought the soul was needed for the next life. The rest of the organs were preserved separately. They were placed in the burial tomb with the body.

3   The body was then filled with stuffing that would help it keep its natural shape. Next, it was covered in *natron*, a natural salt. Natron was used by the Egyptians to draw moisture out of the body. It was important to dry the body out completely so that it would not decay.

4   After 40 to 50 days, the old stuffing was removed and replaced with sawdust or linen. The body was then dabbed with oils and wrapped in strips of cloth. Sometimes, gems and small charms were placed in between layers. Finally, the last layer, the shroud, was placed over the wrapped mummy, and it was moved to a *sarcophagus*. The sarcophagus was a stone or wood box.

5   Not everyone was mummified. It was an honor set aside for the wealthy and for *pharaohs*, or Egyptian kings. Pharaohs were looked at as gods. Their sarcophaguses were often decorated to look like them. Some even had gold details.

6   Important objects were placed in mummies' tombs. Bodies were buried with jewelry, treasures, games, food, and even beloved pets. The Egyptians wanted to be sure that the dead were buried with everything they would need in the afterlife. Many Egyptian pharaohs were buried in stone *pyramids*. Their bodies have been preserved for up to 5,000 years! The exploration of mummies has given today's humans a snapshot at what life was once like long ago.

Guided Practice Drawing Inferences

I. Why did the ancient Egyptians sometimes include gems and charms between layers of cloth on a mummy?

> The answer to this question cannot be found directly in the text. However, there is evidence in the text that helps you arrive at an answer. The text states that the ancient Egyptians believed that people would need objects in the afterlife. It also states that only wealthy and powerful people were mummified. You probably know that *gems* are stones such as diamonds and rubies that are often worth a lot of money. *Charms* are jewelry or decorations that might be made from gold or other precious metals. Putting all the evidence together, you can draw the inference that some mummies included gems and charms because the people had been wealthy in life and it was believed they could use treasured objects like gems and charms in the afterlife.

Now, answer the question in your own words.

_____

_____

2. How are real Egyptian mummies similar to and different from mummies seen in cartoons, Halloween costumes, and movies?

> First, think about mummies you have seen in cartoons and around Halloween. You know that they are usually people covered in strips of cloth. They walk around in scary or funny ways and sometimes talk. Now, look at evidence from the text. It tells you that mummies were wrapped in strips of cloth, so that detail matches the cartoons. However, the text also tells you that mummies had their organs removed. They were dried out and completely lifeless. Real mummies could not walk or talk. Using all this evidence, you can draw an inference to answer the question.

Answer the question in your own words.

_____

_____

_____

Independent Practice Drawing Inferences

1. Would a worker who helped build a pyramid in ancient Egypt likely be mummified after death? Why or why not?

_____

_____

2. What might happen to a person's liver during mummification?

_____

_____

3. What did ancient Egyptians value most?
   A. pets   **B.** the heart
   C. pyramids   **D.** success in the afterlife

4. Ancient Egyptian mummies could best be described as
   A. dry.   **B.** charmed.
   C. decorated.   **D.** kingly.

5. Ancient Egyptian pyramids could best be described as
   A. vacation spots.   **B.** treasures.
   C. tombs.   **D.** palaces.

6. What would not be found in an ancient Egyptian pyramid?
   A. a mummy   **B.** a sarcophagus
   C. treasures   **D.** a wristwatch

7. Archaeologists often find objects left behind from ancient cultures, including pots, jewelry, coins, and buildings. How are mummies different from these?

_____

_____

_____

Informational Text Finding the Main Idea

Read the text. Use it to answer the questions on pages 15 and 16.

Every Drop Counts

1   Turn on the faucet. Wash your hands, or fill up a glass of water. Go swimming at the pool. Take a long, hot shower. Water the garden. Many Americans don't think much about using water. We know that it's a good idea not to waste water. Many people turn off the water while they brush their teeth. Some people collect rainwater to use in their gardens. Even so, most people take for granted that water will always be available. If you live in California, though, you may think about water differently. People there have learned a lesson that many others have not. Water is a precious resource, one that we all need to learn to conserve.

2   California gets some of its water from the Sierra Nevada Mountains. When the snowpack on the mountains melts in the spring, it fills up lakes and rivers. The problem is that in recent years, there hasn't been much snow in the mountains. The lakes and streams aren't filling up. As a result, California has experienced several *droughts*, or extreme water shortages. The state is in danger of running out of fresh water.

3   For the first time, California has placed *mandatory*, or not voluntary, limits on water use. These are laws that citizens and companies have to follow. If they don't, they could be fined. Even with these limits, more change is needed. People cannot keep using water the way they have been. There just isn't enough of it in parts of the United States.

4   One solution is to replace large areas of grass in California. Grass needs a lot of water. Plants that can tolerate drought are a better choice. People are encouraged to do the same with their lawns. With water limits, Californians can water only two days a week. Watering after storms also isn't allowed. Water companies are charging more for water. If people have to pay more, they may use their water more carefully.

5   California isn't the only state with water problems. Many other states are also experiencing droughts. As global climate change brings warmer temperatures to many parts of the world, we may see more water shortages. Water is a valuable resource. No life can exist without it. The sooner we all learn to conserve water, the sooner we will have enough for everyone.

NAME _____

Guided Practice Finding the Main Idea

1. "If you live in California, though, you may think about water differently." Does this statement give the main idea of the text on page 14? Why or why not?

> To answer this question, look carefully at the statement given. It mentions California, and you know the text talks a lot about that state. It also mentions water, and you know that water conservation is the topic of the text. So, at first glance, it seems like it might be the main idea, or most important idea, of the text. Take a closer look at the question and at evidence from the text. The statement given is about Californians and their way of thinking about water. Is the entire text about Californians? No. The text mentions other states as well, and it talks about why water is important to all people. The statement says that some people "may think about water differently." Does it tell what people think about water? Does it tell why thinking about water is important? No. It does not give a main idea about why water conservation is important.

Answer the question in your own words.

_____

_____

_____

2. How does the title "Every Drop Counts" relate to the main idea of the text on page 14?

> You know the topic of the text is water shortage and conservation. The main idea of the text could be stated like this: Water is a very valuable resource that must be carefully conserved by everyone. Does the title "Every Drop Counts" reinforce this main idea? Yes. "Every drop" refers to water, even a very small amount of it. "Counts" means that water matters. "Every Drop Counts" sums up the main idea of the text because it gives the message that people should value and conserve every drop of water.

Now, answer the question in your own words.

_____

_____

Spectrum Focus: Reading for Main Ideas and Details
Grade 4

Guided Practice

15

Independent Practice Finding the Main Idea

1. The main idea of a text is the most important idea that the author wants you to understand and remember. Circle words that relate to the main idea of the text on page 14.

drought   flood   water

state   valuable   conserve

2. Which sentence from the text on page 14 is the best statement of the main idea?

   A. California isn't the only state with water problems.

   B. If people have to pay more, they may use their water more carefully.

   C. Many Americans don't think much about using water.

   D. Water is a precious resource, one that we all need to learn to conserve.

3. Write the main idea of the text on page 14 in your own words.

   _____

   _____

4. In many informational texts, the main idea is restated near the end, often in the last paragraph. Write a sentence from paragraph 5 on page 14 that restates the main idea.

   _____

   _____

5. Which would not make a good title for the text on page 14?

   A. Water: Our Most Precious Resource

   B. Down From the Mountains

   C. California Teaches Us All a Lesson

   D. Not a Drop to Waste

6. The main idea of "Every Drop Counts" is important for

   A. Californians.   **B.** everyone who uses water.

   C. farmers.   **D.** Americans.

NAME _____

Informational Text Finding Key Details

Read the text. Use it to answer the questions on pages 18 and 19.

Play with Your Food!

1   It's hard to imagine preparing a bagel or a pea in a way that would make it seem totally new and different. However, a chef named Nathan Myhrvold is doing just that. Myhrvold makes tasty dishes by using technology to cook familiar foods in surprising ways.

2   Myhrvold did not start out as a chef. In fact, he has college degrees in physics and economics. He spent years working for the computer company Microsoft. It is his background in science and technology that gives Myhrvold a new twist on food.

3   Myhrvold's work happens as much in the lab as it does in the kitchen. He uses what he knows about science to think about food in unusual ways. As he creates new recipes, he tries to understand what makes up food and why it behaves the way it does. Not all his experiments work, but he always learns something new.

4   Myhrvold uses machines you don't often see in kitchens. For example, he is a fan of cooking with a *centrifuge*. A centrifuge is a machine that spins materials at a very high speed. It can be used to separate foods into layers, which is how Myhrvold makes pea butter. First, he purees, or blends, the peas. Then, he puts them in a centrifuge. It separates the pea puree into three layers: starch, juice, and a thin layer of fat. It takes more than a pound of peas to make just a few bites of pea butter. The flavor is intense. People say that it captures the exact nature of peas.

5   Myhrvold is known for all kinds of interesting meals. Would you try a bagel in a glass? Myhrvold makes a liquid "everything" bagel. It must feel strange to sip a food that is usually firm and chewy! Another dish is "spaghetti" with clam sauce. What makes it different is that the noodles are made of clams! Myhrvold uses a machine to pound the clams until they are soft enough to make into noodles. Then, he uses a centrifuge to make sauce from clams, too!

6   If you're interested in Myhrvold's recipes, it will cost you. His 2,400-page cookbook costs a whopping $625. Many experts think it is worth the price. Nothing like it has ever been written before. It may not be for everyone, but there's no doubt that Myhrvold is changing the way people think about food!

NAME_____

Guided Practice Finding Key Details

1. "Play with Your Food!" states that Myhrvold uses technology to cook. Which is a key detail that supports this statement?

   A. Myhrvold has a college degree in physics.

   B. Myhrvold is a fan of cooking with a centrifuge.

   C. Myhrvold cooks familiar foods in surprising ways.

   D. Myhrvold purees peas.

   > To answer this question, compare each choice to the idea given in the question, "Myhrvold uses technology to cook." In order to support this statement, a key detail will be about both technology and cooking. Detail A relates to science and technology, but not to cooking. Detail B mentions cooking with a centrifuge. You know from reading the text that a centrifuge is a high-tech machine. Details C and D are about cooking, but not about technology.

   Now, circle a letter above to answer the question.

2. What key detail from paragraph 5 supports the main idea of the text on page 17? Why?

   > Paragraph 5 contains many details. Which one is a *key detail* that best supports the main idea? To decide, first find the main idea of the entire text. It is found at the end of paragraph 1: "Myhrvold makes tasty dishes by using technology to cook familiar foods in surprising ways." Now, reread paragraph 5. It describes two of Myhrvold's recipes—liquid bagels and spaghetti with clam sauce. These are both examples of the "tasty dishes" mentioned in the main idea. Is there a key detail that ties both of these examples together? Yes. The first sentence of paragraph 5 does that. It must be a key idea.

   Now, answer the question. Use complete sentences.

   _____

   _____

   _____

NAME _____

Independent Practice Finding Key Details

1. Underline the most important detail in the paragraph below. Then, explain how it supports the main idea "Myhrvold makes tasty dishes by using technology to cook familiar foods in surprising ways."

> 2   Myhrvold did not start out as a chef. In fact, he has college degrees in physics and economics. He spent years working for the computer company Microsoft. It is his background in science and technology that gives Myhrvold a new twist on food.

_____

_____

_____

2. Circle the letter beside a key detail from the text on page 17.

A. Myhrvold can prepare peas and bagels in ways that make them seem new and different.

B. Myhrvold wrote a cookbook that costs $625.

C. Myhrvold used to work for Microsoft.

D. Myhrvold makes spaghetti with clam sauce.

3. "Play with Your Food!" states that Myhrvold cooks familiar foods in surprising ways. Complete the chart below with details from the text that support this statement.

Familiar Food	Surprising Cooking Method
Peas	
"Everything" Bagel	
Spaghetti with Clam Sauce	

Informational Text Explaining Events

Read the text. Use it to answer the questions on pages 21 and 22.

The Water Cycle

The amount of water on Earth stays the same. It just takes different forms as it moves through the water cycle.

Condensation occurs when water vapor in Earth's atmosphere gets cold. It turns back into little droplets of water and forms clouds.

Precipitation happens when so much water has condensed that the air can't hold it anymore. Rain or snow falls from the clouds. The precipitation lands on bodies of water and on land. Then, the water cycle begins again.

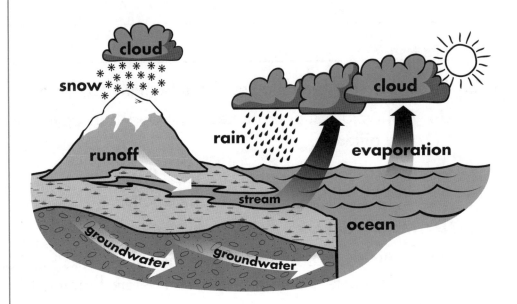

Evaporation happens when the sun heats up water in lakes, oceans, streams, and puddles. It turns into vapor or steam. This water vapor rises up from the body of water into the air.

Guided Practice Explaining Events

1. How does groundwater move through the water cycle? Explain.

To answer this question, scan the diagram on page 20 for the label *groundwater*. Study how groundwater is shown in the diagram. In which direction does the arrow from groundwater point in the cycle? If you need to, read the text around the diagram to better understand each stage in the water cycle. Now, you are ready to write an explanation of how groundwater fits into the cycle of evaporation, condensation, and precipitation. Mention each one of these stages in your answer.

Answer the question in your own words. Use complete sentences.

_____

_____

_____

_____

2. What are clouds? Explain.

To answer this question, find the word *cloud* in two places: in the diagram and in the surrounding text. If there are arrows near the clouds in the diagram, which way are they pointing? What is happening directly below the clouds? Put this information together with information you find in the text about clouds. Now you are ready to answer the question. Make sure to mention each stage in the water cycle and how it relates to clouds.

Answer the question in your own words. Use complete sentences.

_____

_____

_____

_____

Independent Practice Explaining Events

1. When Earth's atmosphere is very cold, precipitation might take the form of

   A. snow.   **B.** rain.

   C. clouds.   **D.** groundwater.

2. Water vapor rises from

   A. oceans.   **B.** streams.

   C. lakes.   **D.** all of the above.

3. Rainwater that falls on the ground and runs toward bodies of water is called

   A. condensation.   **B.** groundwater.

   C. melt.   **D.** runoff.

4. Large clouds contain

   A. a small amount of condensed water.   **B.** runoff.

   C. a large amount of condensed water.   **D.** evaporation.

5. In winter, some water turns to ice. Explain how water that is ice moves through the water cycle.

   _____

   _____

   _____

6. Some soil contains pesticides and other chemicals. Explain what might happen to these chemicals when rainwater falls on the soil.

   _____

   _____

7. What happens to precipitation that falls on mountaintops and other high places? Explain.

   _____

   _____

Informational Text Summarizing

Read the text. Use it to answer the questions below and on page 24.

The Dinosaur Who Feared Nothing

1   In 2005, a new dinosaur specimen was found in Argentina. It is a relative of *Brachiosaurus*. This dino, however, is much bigger than its cousin. In fact, it might be one of the biggest land animals ever!

2   The new dinosaur is named *Dreadnoughtus*. Its name means "fear nothing." It stood about 30 feet tall, or as tall as a three-story building. It was a whopping 85 feet long. This giant weighed about 65 tons, about seven times as much as *T. rex*.

3   Scientists did not figure all of this out right away. They found only about 200 bones of *Dreadnoughtus*, less than half of the dino's skeleton. Luckily, that was enough to let scientists draw many conclusions. The team relied on computers to form an image of what the whole dinosaur looked like. Scientists used 3-D printing to model the creature. They printed bones that haven't yet been found! This helped them learn more about the animal, how it lived, and how it moved. Their work helps all of us understand a little bit more about dinosaurs.

Guided Practice Summarizing

A summary includes the most important information from a text. It leaves out less important details. To find the most important information from the text above, complete the chart with evidence from the text.

Who or what is the text about?	It is about the dinosaur *Dreadnoughtus*.
What information is most important?	1. _____
When does something important happen?	2. _____
Where does something important happen?	3. _____
Why is this topic important?	This topic is important because each new dinosaur discovery helps us learn more about dinosaurs.
How does something important happen?	Scientists used computers and 3-D printers to help them model *Dreadnoughtus*.

Spectrum Focus: Reading for Main Ideas and Details
Grade 4

Independent Practice Summarizing

1. On the lines below, write a summary of "The Dinosaur Who Feared Nothing."
   Write in complete sentences using your own words. Use the completed chart
   on page 23 to help you. Include only the most important information from the
   text. Leave out less important details. Your summary should be short—use only
   the lines provided below.

   _____

   _____

   _____

   _____

   _____

2. Reread the summary you wrote. Did you include only the most important
   information? On the lines below, explain why or why not. If you included
   non-important details in your summary, cross them out.

   _____

   _____

   _____

3. Now, compare your summary to the completed chart on page 23. Did you
   include all the information from the chart in your summary? On the lines
   below, explain why or why not. If you need to, add more information to the
   summary you wrote above.

   _____

   _____

   _____

Performance Task

Read the texts. Use them to complete each step of the task that follows.

Biggest Natural Disasters in U.S. History	
Blizzard	The Great Blizzard of 1888 swept across the northeastern United States, bringing 40–50 inches of snow. The storm caused 400 deaths and the sinking of 200 ships in the Atlantic Ocean.
Earthquake	An earthquake at Rat Islands, Alaska, in 1965 had a magnitude of 8.7. It triggered massive landslides and a 30-foot tsunami that reached Hawaii. Because the area was remote, only 131 deaths occurred.
Hurricane	The Great Galveston Hurricane of 1900 hit the Texas coastline on September 8. It brought a storm surge of 8–15 feet and caused 8,000–12,000 deaths.
Tornado	In March, 1925, the Tri-State Tornado struck in Missouri, Illinois, and Indiana. The giant twister caused 695 deaths.

Name the Storm

1. What is a rapidly spinning column of air that touches both a cloud above and the ground below?
2. What is a severe snowstorm with winds greater than 35 miles per hour?
3. What happens when plates of rock shift and break beneath Earth's surface?
4. What spiraling storm gathers heat and energy from warm ocean waters?

1. a tornado; 2. a blizzard; 3. an earthquake; 4. a hurricane

Emergency Preparedness

People in every part of the U.S. need to be prepared for natural disasters. Each family should have a disaster plan that includes escape routes and safe places to meet. At least one family member should be trained in first aid. Having an emergency kit on hand is crucial. It should contain water, non-perishable food, flashlights, spare batteries, blankets, and copies of important documents. During a hurricane, cover windows and doorways with plywood and be prepared to evacuate. If conditions are right for a tornado, seek shelter in a basement, protected interior room, or low-lying area. To protect yourself from an earthquake, get under a sturdy piece of furniture and hang on tightly. During blizzards and other winter storms, seek shelter inside. If stranded outside, build a snow cave to block high winds.

Performance Task

Read each main idea and write key details from the texts on page 25 to support it. For #3, write a main idea of your own and support it with details from the texts.

1. Main Idea: *Storms can be powerful and deadly.*

   Detail: _____

   _____

   Detail: _____

   _____

2. Main Idea: *Seeking shelter is important to surviving natural disasters.*

   Detail: _____

   _____

   Detail: _____

   _____

3. Main Idea: _____

   Detail: _____

   _____

   Detail: _____

   _____

Answer the following questions in complete sentences.

4. Which types of storms are likely to cause flooding? Why?

   _____

   _____

5. What might happen if windows and doorways are not covered during a hurricane?

   _____

   _____

Performance Task

6. During an earthquake, what is happening above the surface of Earth?

_____

_____

7. Use the texts on page 25. Write a brief summary of what you have learned about natural disasters in the U.S.

_____

_____

_____

_____

8. Imagine you have been asked to write a flyer explaining what families should know about natural disasters and how they can prepare. The flyer will be distributed to people who visit a community health and safety fair. First, review the rubric below. Then, use the space on page 28 to design and write your flyer. Include a title or slogan that gives the main idea. Support your main idea with key details. If you wish, include illustrations.

	Proficient	**Learning**	**Beginner**
Main Idea	A title or slogan gives a clear main idea about why it is important to know about natural disasters and prepare for them.	A title or slogan gives a somewhat clear main idea about why it is important to know about natural disasters and prepare for them.	A title or slogan does not give a main idea about why it is important to know about natural disasters and prepare for them.
Key Details	Many key details support the main idea.	Some key details support the main idea.	Few key details support the main idea.
Explaining Procedures and Ideas	The flyer gives a complete explanation of how to recognize natural disasters and be prepared for them.	The flyer gives a somewhat complete explanation of how to recognize natural disasters and be prepared for them.	The flyer gives an incomplete explanation of how to recognize natural disasters and be prepared for them.

Performance Task

Front:

Back:

Now, use the rubric on page 27 to evaluate your flyer. For each topic, circle *Proficient, Learning,* or *Beginner*. This will help you know what skills you need to work on.

Assessment

Read the text. Use it to answer the questions that follow.

Printing the Future

1   Technology is always changing the world. Think of the Internet, cell phones, and digital cameras. Today, these devices are part of daily life. Soon, three-dimensional printers, or *3-D printers*, may be something we take for granted, too. Three-dimensional printers are likely to change the world in many ways.

2   A 3-D printer can make, or print, objects that have length, width, and height. In other words, it prints real objects instead of two-dimensional pictures on paper. 3-D printers use all kinds of materials to make things. Plastic is used most often. Other materials, such as rubber, metal, and even food, can also fill their cartridges.

3   The printer uses a design that the user provides. The design tells the printer what to do—how to build the object. Then, the printer goes to work. It builds the object from scratch. With the simple press of a button, you can print a necklace, a vase, a toy, or a candy bar.

4   3-D printers could be useful in many ways. Imagine that a part of your bike breaks. You could print out a copy of the broken piece at home. Teachers might use the printers to make learning materials. Artists could make sculptures. Factories could print shoes, airplane propellers, or dishes. There is almost no limit to what these amazing printers might do.

5   Someday, 3-D printers may bring great advances to the world of medicine. Today, if a patient needs a new heart, he or she has to wait until one is available for transplant. In the future, 3-D printers may be able to print out organs that people need. Printers might also be used to make new limbs, joints, medicine, and medical devices.

6   Lots of new issues are sure to develop because of 3-D printers. For example, how will copyright be handled? A *copyright* gives ownership of an idea or object to the person who invented it. What will happen when people can easily print their own things at home? Another problem is how 3-D printers might affect jobs. Today, machines do many jobs humans used to do. Will 3-D printers take over more jobs?

7   The world is changing quickly, and 3-D printers are a part of that change. How will they make the world a better place? It's exciting to think of all the ways 3-D printers may change our lives in the future.

NAME _____

Assessment

Part 1: I can find details to answer questions.

1. The material most often used by 3-D printers is
   - **A.** metal.
   - **B.** plastic.
   - **C.** paper.
   - **D.** clay.

2. A 3-D printer
   - **A.** uses a design provided by the user.
   - **B.** prints pictures on paper.
   - **C.** has not yet been invented.
   - **D.** is something most people take for granted.

3. Describe three ways in which 3-D printers may someday improve people's lives.

   _____

   _____

   _____

4. How are 3-D printers the same as 2-D printers? How are they different?

   _____

   _____

   _____

Part 2: I can draw inferences.

1. What object might be printed using a 3-D printer filled with metal?

   _____

2. Imagine you are an inventor of machine parts. Explain your opinion about 3-D printers.

   _____

   _____

   _____

Assessment

3. Imagine you are a doctor. Explain your opinion about 3-D printers.

_____

_____

_____

Part 3: I can find the main idea and key details of an informational text.

Complete the organizer. First, write the main idea of the entire text on page 29. Then, write one key detail from each paragraph of the text.

1. Main idea: _____

_____

2. Key detail from paragraph 2: _____

_____

3. Key detail from paragraph 3: _____

_____

4. Key detail from paragraph 4: _____

_____

5. Key detail from paragraph 5: _____

_____

6. Key detail from paragraph 6: _____

_____

7. Choose one key detail you wrote in items 2–6. Explain how it supports the main idea of "Printing the Future."

_____

_____

Assessment

Part 4: I can use details to explain events and ideas.

Read the following description of how a 3-D printer works. Cross out two sentences that are not correct.

Load the printer with plastic, rubber, metal, or another material. Turn the printer on. Choose an object that you want to copy and set it on the printer. Download a design to the printer. Press the START button. Feed a sheet of paper into the printer. Wait for your object to print.

Part 5: I can summarize an informational text.

Complete the chart with evidence from the text.

Who or what is the text about?	1. _____
What information is most important?	2. _____
When does something important happen?	3. _____
Where does something important happen?	4. _____
Why is this topic important?	5. _____
How does something important happen?	6. _____

7. On the lines below, write a summary of "Printing the Future" in your own words.

_____

_____

_____

_____

_____

_____

Answer Key

Page 9

1. The two ingredients needed for making bread are flour and water. **2.** One type of bread eaten in Italy is focaccia.

Page 10

1. wheat, oats, rye, cornmeal, millet, quinoa, rice; **2.** Russians eat kulich on Easter, and Mexicans eat pan de muerto on the Day of the Dead. **3.** A type of bread in Singapore, roti jala, gets its name from a fisherman's net because it is full of holes and resembles a net. **4.** B; **5.** yeast, tawa; **6.** Yeast change sugar into other chemicals.

Page 12

1. Some mummies had gems and charms between their layers so that the people could use their valuable items in the afterlife. **2.** Both cartoon mummies and real mummies are wrapped in strips of cloth. Cartoon mummies can walk around and make sounds, but real mummies are not alive and cannot do these things.

Page 13

1. A worker who helped to build the pyramids would not be likely to become a mummy. The text says that only wealthy and powerful people became mummies, and workers are not usually wealthy or powerful. **2.** The text states that the only organ left inside mummies was the heart. The liver is an organ other than the heart. The text states that other organs were preserved separately and buried in the tomb with the mummy. So, the liver would probably be preserved and buried close to the mummy. **3.** D; **4.** A; **5.** C; **6.** D; **7.** Mummies are different from pots, jewelry, and other objects because they are actually preserved bodies from the past.

Page 15

1. The statement is not the main idea. It says that Californians may think about water differently from other people, but it does not talk about all people and the importance of conserving water. The statement is not the main idea because it does not give the most important ideas of the whole text. **2.** The title "Every Drop Counts" is related to the main idea of the text because it says that even one drop of water is important to use wisely, which is the most important idea of the text.

Page 16

1. drought, water, valuable, conserve; **2.** D; **3.** Answers will vary. Possible answer: Everyone needs water, so everyone should use it wisely so there is enough to go around. **4.** The sooner we all learn to conserve water, the sooner we will have enough for everyone. **5.** B; **6.** B

Answer Key

Page 18

1. B; **2.** The key detail *Myhrvold is known for all kinds of interesting meals* supports the main idea of the entire text. It supports the idea that Myhrvold makes a variety of surprising dishes.

Page 19

1. Students should underline the sentence *It is his background in science and technology that gives Myhrvold a new twist on food.* This is a key detail that supports the main idea because it explains why Myhrvold uses technology in his cooking. **2.** A; **3.** Peas: Myrhvold makes pea butter using a centrifuge. "Everything" Bagel: Myrhvold makes solid bagels into liquids. Spaghetti with Clam Sauce: Myrhvold uses a machine to pound clams into noodles and a centrifuge to make clam sauce.

Page 21

1. When rain falls and soaks into the ground, it becomes groundwater. Groundwater moves toward streams, oceans, and other bodies of water. From there, it evaporates into the air as water vapor. Then, the vapor condenses into clouds. When the air can no longer hold all the condensed water, it falls back to Earth as rain or snow. **2.** Clouds are formed when water vapor evaporates into the air, becomes cold, and condenses back into water droplets. These water droplets are clouds. When there is a lot of condensed water in the air, it falls back to Earth as precipitation.

Page 22

1. A; **2.** D; **3.** D; **4.** C; **5.** Water that is ice is trapped on land or in a body of water. When the ice melts, it can evaporate into the air and enter the water cycle. **6.** When rainwater falls on soil that contains chemicals, the chemicals might travel with the rainwater as runoff into nearby streams and lakes or into the ground as groundwater. When the water evaporates, the chemicals might travel into the air and become part of the water cycle. **7.** When rain or snow falls on a mountaintop or another high place, gravity makes it travel down as runoff into lakes, streams, and oceans below where it evaporates into the air to begin the water cycle again.

Page 23

1. The newly discovered dinosaur may have been the biggest land animal ever. **2.** The new dinosaur was discovered in 2005. **3.** The dinosaur was discovered in Argentina.

Page 24

1. Summaries will vary. Sample summary: The dinosaur *Dreadnoughtus* may have been the biggest land animal ever. It was discovered in 2005 in Argentina. Even though not all its bones were found, researchers used computers and 3-D printing to make a model of the animal. This helps us all learn more about dinosaurs. **2.** Answers will vary. **3.** Answers will vary.

Answer Key

Performance Task

1. Answers will vary. Possible answers: The Great Blizzard of 1888 caused 400 deaths. A 1965 earthquake had a magnitude of 8.7. **2.** Answers will vary. Possible answers: During a tornado, the safest place is in a basement, protected room, or low-lying area. If stranded outside during a blizzard, build a snow cave for protection. **3.** Answers will vary. **4.** Hurricanes are likely to cause flooding when they bring huge storms onto land from the ocean. Blizzards are likely to cause flooding when a large amount of snow melts. **5.** If windows and doorways are not covered during a hurricane, water from the storm surge could come inside. **6.** During an earthquake, plates of rock are shifting under Earth's surface. Above Earth's surface, buildings, roads, trees, bodies of water, and anything else on land is being shaken. **7.** Summaries will vary. Possible summary: Four kinds of natural disasters that can occur in the U.S. are blizzards, earthquakes, hurricanes, and tornados. These storms can be powerful and can destroy the environment and cause deaths. It is important to know how to stay safe during a natural disaster. You can be prepared by having emergency supplies and seeking shelter in a safe place. **8.** Flyers will vary. Students should complete the rubric to determine their level of proficiency.

Assessment

Part 1: 1. B; **2.** A; **3.** Answers will vary. Possible answers: They may help teachers create learning materials. They may allow you to print parts to repair things. They may allow doctors to print new organs or medical devices. **4.** Both 2-D printers and 3-D printers make copies of things based on downloaded information or designs. However, 2-D printers print only flat images that have width and height, while 3-D printers create objects that have length, height, and width.

Part 2: 1. Answers will vary. Possible answer: A 3-D printer filled with metal might be used to make a bicycle part. **2.** Answers will vary. Possible answer: I do not want everyone to own a 3-D printer because I don't want everyone to be able to make copies of my inventions for free. When I design something, I have a copyright that means I own the idea behind it. I have the right to make money when one of my inventions is sold. If people can print things for free, they won't buy my inventions. **3.** Answers will vary. Possible answer: I am excited for 3-D printers to be built and improved so that they might someday be able to print human organs and other body parts, medical devices, or medicines. If these things could be easily printed, they would save a lot of lives and improve medical care.

Part 3: 1. Three-dimensional printers are likely to change the world in many ways. **2.** A 3-D printer can make, or print, objects that have length, width, and height. **3.** The printer uses a design that the user provides. **4.** 3-D printers could be useful in many ways. **5.** Someday, 3-D printers may bring great advances to the world of medicine. **6.** Lots of new issues are sure to develop because of 3-D printers. **7.** Answers will vary.

Part 4: Students should cross out the sentences *Choose an object that you want to copy and set it on the printer* and *Feed a sheet of paper into the printer.*

Part 5: 1. The text is about 3-D printers. **2.** Three-dimensional printers may improve people's lives in many ways. **3.** Advances to 3-D printers will happen in the future. **4.** Someday, everyone may have a printer at home. **5.** This topic is important because 3-D printers may someday be used for printing things we need, including artificial organs. **6.** Three-dimensional printers work by making objects from scratch based on users' designs. **7.** Summaries will vary. Possible summary: Three-dimensional printers make objects from scratch based on users' designs. Someday, everyone may own one. In the future, these printers may improve our lives in many ways, giving people the ability to print things they need, even artificial organs.